FOURTH GRADE
My Formative Years

Sebastian J. Payton

authorHOUSE®

AuthorHouse™
1663 Liberty Drive
Bloomington, IN 47403
www.authorhouse.com
Phone: 1-800-839-8640

First published by AuthorHouse 4/5/2010

ISBN: 978-1-4520-0713-7 (e)
ISBN: 978-1-4520-0712-0 (sc)

Library of Congress Control Number: 2010904270

Printed in the United States of America
Bloomington, Indiana

This book is printed on acid-free paper.

Introduction

Teaching has become my life's work. It's been more than a calling. It has been a vehicle for growth. As a man, I am reminded daily by my students that my role is incomparable. As a teacher, I am constantly changing— adapting to the needs of my students, my parents, and my school site. That, in itself, is enough to keep anyone on their toes. Being black is its own animal. I wish that I could say that being black was just another part of the equation, but the reality is that black is the parentheses around the equation. It's the words in the sentence. Being a man and being a teacher are just the capitalization and punctuation in the sentence that says, "I am black."

Being a man is about responsibilities, those that we choose to take, as well as those that we were born to bear. Through teaching I have learned that my responsibility to my own well-being is as important as the job itself. When I learned how to make myself "number one," in my fifth year (fourth grade), my students, my parents, and my peers got the best of me. The significance of this title lies in the fact that it took me that long to fully understand what it meant for me to be a man. I had to give myself the best before I could give anyone else my best!

Teaching has been wonderful, especially with little ones, preschool through third. Teaching is really just another way to say shared learning. I have learned more from my students than they could have ever learned from me. I have had more than two hundred little people walk into my life, and each one of them has taught me a lesson. Most importantly, they have taught me how to take chances and make mistakes.

All of my life my mother and I have been in a continuous conversation about life. We don't always agree. And I hated that because I wanted her to agree with me; I wanted to be right. You know, I didn't always like my mother, but I will always love her for what she did for me! (Does this sound like your relationship with God?)

Like most teachers, she was probably unaware of the impact of all her actions. Through this brief look into my career, you will be given some insight into the character that she built.

Dedications

This book is in tribute to my first and best teacher, my mother, Gwen Payton. My mother raised more than a family, she raised four children—individuals, leaders. And for that, I am eternally, grateful! Every morning, I praise the Lord for what my mother did for me. Momma, this is for you!

A very special thank you goes to James Kelson for being a leader in the community and for giving me my first opportunity.

Thanks to Mr. Daniels for encouraging me to display all of my talents.

Thanks to Mr. and Mrs. Simms who made my student teaching possible.

Thanks to Russ, Molly, and Jaimie for being so supportive in my growth as an educator.

Contents

Part One: Teach 1

Preschool..3
Kindergarten 17
First Grade 31

Part Two: Reteach 43

Second Grade..45
Third Grade 57
Fourth Grade 65

Part One:
Teach

Questions, with no answers ...

Preschool

I THINK I'M A TEACHER, but I'm not sure. What is a teacher? If I don't know what one is, how can I become one?

The first part of my academic career seemed to have no rhyme or reason to it. It began tumultuously. I went to kindergarten at two different schools, because of daycare issues, as far as I know. Second grade saw me be admitted into the gifted/accelerated program. I spent almost four years in the gifted/accelerated program, from second grade through sixth grade. I spent time in speech classes to improve my stuttering problems. I was even involved in a counseling group that was designed to address my behavioral problems, so there are not many services that a public education had to offer that I didn't get a chance to experience. Did I fail to mention that I only spent a week or so in seventh grade before I was promoted to eighth?

Okay, I'll start from the beginning. I grew up in South Phoenix. My mother was the oldest of four. She was a southern girl from Fort Worth, Texas. My father was the oldest of five boys, with one older sister. He was a city boy from the North Philadelphia area. My birth was miraculous, because as far as my mother knew, she was unable to have any more children. I even came early. My first couple of months in this world was tough. I struggled to keep down food, and I had a pretty tough bout with pneumonia. An inauspicious beginning, considering the fact that I grew to be a six-foot-five-inch college basketball player.

Needless to say, my mother and father kept a close eye on my development. By the time I started kindergarten, I knew how to read, write, and problem solve, so kindergarten was spent being a teacher's aide. First grade was a little different. I began to get into trouble. By second grade, I was a fully developed behavioral problem. I would finish all my work and then I would begin to tease, disrupt, and hit my classmates. Fortunately, the district tested me and determined that I was "gifted."

The teacher I had for second and third grade was one of my favorites and one of the best. It was a multi-aged classroom for first through third graders, the primary gifted and accelerated class. It was the only one of its kind in the district. Here I excelled and grew. I performed, "I Have A Dream," I wrote a report on Walter Payton, and I genuinely enjoyed school. But it would be short-lived. The following year, someone I knew joined the class—my little sister! Remember, this was a multi-aged classroom, and my sister had just become a first grader.

We proceeded to dominate the classroom, academically and emotionally. We were so strong and required so much attention that we consumed our class. After having been awarded nearly every type of academic recognition that the school had to offer, my mother was informed that it would be in the best interest of the school to keep my sister and me separated academically. This would prove to be a devastating blow to my development. Not only did the program change sites the next year, but I was also in a less dynamic classroom.

Fourth and fifth grade saw me back in trouble. It was a constant parade in and out of the office for swats, corporal punishment, and detention. Outside of receiving a certificate for "most yelled at in one year," which I still have, I don't remember anything good about the time in school, except for playing the sousaphone in marching band. In sixth grade, I had a phenomenal teacher, who got to me through Scrabble, but that year was marred by counseling services for impulsive and aggressive behavior.

By seventh grade, things had changed. I had grown to be six feet tall, and I was in a regular classroom. For some reason, I was not placed in the gifted/accelerated program. Well, it didn't take long for me to get bored and get into trouble. I got in trouble with a music teacher who I thought was strange.

He sent me to the office, where I was to be swatted three times or something like that. I forget; it's been a while! As the principal began to hit me, he missed and hit my hip. On the second swat, he missed again. Before he could swing again, I took his paddle and threatened to hit him back. With his diminutive stature, five-foot-two or so, you can imagine how intimidating I might have been, even back then. This combined with my past poor behavior made his decision easy. I was expelled immediately and was sent back to my home school. The expulsion didn't bother me. I was going home to be with all of my friends. In retrospect, it could be seen as the right thing to do or as just another poor response to an exceptional child; you can decide after I get out of "preschool."

There has never been a time during my education that I felt like a regular student. Maybe that's because I wasn't a regular student. I can remember kindergarten like it was yesterday. I helped the other students. I helped them with their ABCs and numbers. I can't begin to tell you what I learned in kindergarten or first grade, for that matter.

At least the gifted/accelerated program allowed me to explore my interests. But was I being taught there? Yes and no! In this program, I was being supervised. It was like an academic playground, and I learned how to play everything! I excelled in math and the arts. But, now I was back in a regular education class, at my home school, for the first time since kindergarten!

While at my new school, my home school, I was up to no good. During the preparation for a district pretest, I began to mouth off to my first and only male classroom teacher before high school. I told him that it would be a joke to take this test and that I would breeze through it. He responded to me by telling me that if I didn't pass it, I would be going to the office, so he made me take it before everyone else did. Of course, I aced it and was sent to the office.

Later that day, during shop class, bored out of my mind, I was goofing off with a couple of my classmates when the bell rang to go to the next class. Our instructor kept us over, and I thought for sure that we were going to get into trouble. Well instead, we received a lecture on academic conduct.

Somewhat mystified, he asked me to remain. Sure to be written up, as I slouched in my seat, I turned uninterestedly away. He said, "You're one of the smartest niggers that I have ever met!" With my mouth wide open, I sat up and stared. He proceeded to ramble on about how he wanted to help get me out of the "hood" and send me to a "good" catholic high school. Though I didn't pay attention to all of the details, I remember the feeling of confusion that I experienced.

In all of my life, no one other than my family had ever tried to help me get better it seemed, but this guy does? Why would someone trying to help me call me a name at the same time? It was one of the most contradictory situations I ever went through. At the age of twelve, I was able to shake it off and move on and finish the day.

When I got home, I had to tell my mother that I had gotten in trouble, but when she heard what that man had said, she made it a point to talk to the principal the next day. The teacher was called in, and when he was questioned, he did something unbelievable. He didn't try to conceal what he had called me. In fact, he repeated the statement verbatim. He also reiterated how incredibly bright and talented he thought I was and how he wanted to get me a scholarship. He was released immediately! After a few more test and discussions, I was moved to the eighth grade.

Even now, I still hold no ill-will toward that man. After all, is he any worse than a teacher who gives you the "Most Yelled at in One Year" certificate? I'll tell you what, when I think about what he did, I laugh at his boldness. When I think about what she did, I don't smile at all. You know, I saw her when I got my first teaching job. The first thing she said was, "I thought that you were going to be in jail!" Ain't nothin' funny about that!

I went from being a seventh grader in a regular classroom at one school, to being expelled at that same school, to being in seventh grade at my home school in another regular class, to a being an eighth grader in a matter of weeks. That was when I learned that there are no teachers in school, just students. They may be older. And in my experience, they may not even be bigger. I think I taught that shop teacher more than he taught me, because I'm still not very handy and he lost his job. Who was the teacher and who was the student? You tell me!

Once I got through eighth grade, I was off to high school. It was a blur academically. My grades were mediocre at best. My behavior was better, but only because of basketball, at least until sophomore year. During that year, I had a competition with one of my buddies. We wanted to see who could sustain the longest streak of missing homework assignments and still get good test grades, B or higher! Our mothers knew each other, and his mother found out first; then she told my mother to check for my homework. Well, I won the contest, but the cost was high. My mother took me off the team because of it and told me that me that I had to rededicate myself to the schoolwork. I had learned my lesson, compliments of my mother and my math teacher, whom I really liked. Consequences are never predictable! I didn't miss another homework assignment. But I did miss the rest of the season!

After that year, we moved out of the "projects" and into a house that my brother owned on the other side of town. My last two years in high school were spent at a different school. Those years were just as inconsistent as any other time. My last two years athletically included a stellar junior year in basketball, followed by a dismissal from the team as a senior and team state championship in track and field. Additionally, I was recognized as the Youth of the Year for the state of Arizona. Finally, I was elected as the boys' state governor and participated in Model U.N. as a delegate. I learned a great deal during this time. However, much of it took place outside of the classroom.

At seventeen years of age, I began school on a full basketball scholarship to a junior college in northern Arizona. The scenery was different, and so was the structure. At this point, I had formed some strong opinions about how the world worked, so I was a little angry to say the least. My first day of school didn't help. As I entered my first collegiate math class, pre-calculus, I was excited. Math had always been my favorite subject, and as a pre-engineering major, I knew that it would be an integral to my career as a civil engineer.

As I searched for a seat in the back, the instructor said to me, "General math is down the hall!" Maybe it was my basketball shorts. Maybe it was my height. Maybe it was my color, or maybe it was a combination of them all! Nevertheless, armed with a sharp wit, a ghetto mentality, and a little arrogance, I fired back, "I know. I just walked one of my teammates over there. That's my name right there on your roster, 'Sebastian J. Payton,' and I'm sittin' right here in front of you! I'm gonna get an A in this class, too!" I received an A- in that class. I wonder why? Well, now I knew why Public Enemy made that song about Arizona.

Again, my grades were somewhat mediocre for the first two years. Even though I was really interested in becoming an engineer, it hadn't inspired me to excel. Interestingly, whenever I wasn't practicing or studying, I was tutoring. I had become fairly good at it too. My "students" routinely outscored me on tests, and I didn't mind. In fact, I enjoyed it.

In my second year of college, it hit me one morning. After learning that yet another person had outscored me on a test that I had tutored him on, I realized that I wasn't angry about it. After all, I had helped him, and I was genuinely happy for my teammate. As I searched my past, I realized that all of my experiences had been preparing me for a different career.

So after a few conversations with my mentor, himself a civil engineer, and some heavy thought, I decided that teaching would be a better field for me. My life experience had involved coaching, tutoring, and a love for children, so for me it just made sense. But I was only nineteen, and I guess that's not the age of maturity, because my family didn't agree with my decision. Here I was nineteen years old, and people were still trying to tell me what to do, as if I didn't know any better.

Even my mother, of all people, urged me to change my major. I think that she thought that I was taking the easy way out, with respect to the academic rigor. That was hard for me because this decision was definitely an act of faith, and my mother was a major reason why I had such faith in God. It seemed to me that her life had been one big exercise in faith, so I was only emulating the only lifestyle that I had ever been exposed to, a lifestyle based on faith. Well, I didn't care if had their support. I did it. I changed my major from engineering to education.

Three months later I would make the most important move of my life! I would choose to go to a private Christian school to finish my undergraduate degree. GC was located in the upper middle class town of Wenham, in Massachusetts. I would be one of only four African Americans on a campus of about eleven hundred. Before I go on, let me say this: black is not all that I am, but it is who I am, among other things! Nothing made that more obvious to me than my experiences at this new school.

When I arrived I was slapped in the face with a greeting of good old-fashioned prejudice. Jet-lagged and cold, I arrived at the quaint campus. A greeter directed me to the registrar's office. After filling out paperwork, I was directed to the orientation. On the way there, I was approached by a female student. We greeted each other, and we walked and talked a bit. While we were walking, she asked me something weird. She asked if I was a member of the choir. I knew nothing about the choir, so I told her no. Puzzled, I asked her, "Why?" She responded that someone had told her that I was a choir member. I responded that no one at the school knew me well enough to know if I could sing at all, even though I can sing! Then she remarked that I must have been on the basketball team. Jokingly, I told her that I was on the soccer team. Obviously embarrassed, she walked away. And I was reminded again, as I was in my first college situation, how important being black was to everybody else, including black people!

My first lesson came from a sociology professor with whom I had my first philosophical disagreement. This was a monumental event for me for two reasons. First, he was my first black male college instructor, the only black male instructor I had ever had. Second, he forced me to study my culture on a deeper level. For the first time in my life, someone was attempting to teach me in the classroom. We had several disagreements about vocabulary and content philosophy with respect to race and ethnicity. Every response paper that I wrote was usually based on a philosophical disagreement I had with a lecture, and each one of them was given a poor grade, with one exception.

I did a joint project/presentation with another student. Our presentation received an A, but our paper received an interesting grade. For me it received a D and for her it received an A. When I went in to speak to him about it, he told me that her grade was none of my business but that the paper was poorly done. From that point on, he made public reference to my unwillingness to accept his doctrine every chance he got. And even though he gave me my first and only D, he still tried to teach to me. However unsuccessful, he did teach me something about being a teacher: "You cannot teach if you are unwilling to learn."

My second lesson also came from a sociology instructor; sociology was my second major. During a classroom debate, I had impressed my professor, which wasn't such a big deal, except I was not doing as well in this class as I might have hoped. After class, he spoke to me and offered me some advice in the form of a question, "Why isn't all of your work this passionate?" He also emphasized that the clarity and quality of my presentations were in direct contrast to my written work, which was lackluster at best. I responded to him immediately through my work. By the end of the semester, my grades had improved, and he gave me a book, along with some encouragement, "One day you will be at the highest level of academia. The only thing that will separate you from the others will be your passion." And so I learned that it's okay to exhibit love in what you do.

This next lesson was very subtle, and it too came from a sociology professor. Are you sensing a theme here? I wasn't! All I knew about this experience was that it was okay that I didn't understand it. While in class, I presented a compelling argument on social status in the United States. Subsequently, I wrote a paper on it. The presentation received a high A, but the paper received a low C. When I went in to see him about it, he was very direct: "You speak like a professor, but you write like a high school student. If you can't put it in writing, then you'll never be able to share your ideas effectively!"(Point taken!)

My last lesson was the toughest and the most important. After all my classes on lesson plans, theory, and classroom management, my professor and I mapped out a student teaching experience. Half of my student-teaching would take place in a preschool setting, and the other half of it would take place in a traditional kindergarten setting. I had completed the first part, and I only had one week in the kindergarten. Then one day, in the midst of a New England winter, I was called into my advisor's office, I thought to be prepped on my final week before completion of my education program. Instead I was in for the shock of my life.

He brought me in and told me that I would not be completing my program and that tomorrow would be my last day in that classroom. Angry and confused, I left! How was I going to tell my little five-year-old students that I was not going to return? Still stunned and unclear about what was going on, I went to the classroom and told my a.m. and p.m. classes that I would not be coming back. Teary-eyed and sad, they hugged me and said their good-byes!

Later on that day, during my lunch, the principal of the school shared that she thought that I was better suited for business or possibly older students. Keep in mind that I had never met this woman and that I couldn't recall ever seeing her in my classroom while I was there for any significant amount of time. My supervising teacher said that I was unprepared and unprofessional. Already a little shaky after talking with my advisor the night before, I was devastated!

I was sad, angry, and confused. Needless to say, my emotions were all over the place. After about an hour of crying in my snowy, frozen car, I went to my advisor for a more thorough explanation. In a chilling tone, he told me that I wasn't ready to teach, because of a lack of content knowledge. Nobody had their story straight. Was it content, professionalism, or was I simply in the wrong field? It didn't matter; consistency wouldn't have brought me much comfort. All I knew was that my dream had been deferred. I went to my room and sat in the dark for hours. I could have killed that day. All of my dreams destroyed by an opinion! I praise the Lord every day that I've never owned a weapon, because that man would have probably been dead!

Several hours later, I called my family to tell them the news. I called my mother. She was surprised too but for a different reason. She wanted to know how I could have been so careless to make a mistake now. Despite my pleas of innocence, she condemned me to guilt. Finally, she put her feelings aside and offered to speak to the school on my behalf. I rejected her assistance.

I took my case to the dean of education. He told me that he respected the opinion of my advisor because he was so well respected in the educational community, even though the facts were inconsistent. After a long and fruitless appeal process, I left that institution with a sociology degree and a bunch of empty, useless credit hours in general studies, not to mention the tuition that was wasted. But now I was more focused than ever!

I came home not dejected but determined. So I worked and went to school, this time not focused on grades, classes or instructors, but rather the experiences, the dialogue, and my classmates. Interestingly enough, I received mostly As. So about a year after coming home, I had completed my coursework and I finally became a certified elementary school teacher.

In all my years in school, there is not one class that taught me how to be a teacher; rather, my life experiences shaped the teacher that I am and will be! I became a teacher in response to what I considered to be a poor education. My teachers weren't bad teachers; they were just products of bad teachers. By that I mean that most of my teachers taught a subject matter and not individuals. In school, I learned how to solve problems, starting with my own!

I can do all things through Christ which strengtheneth me (Phil. 4:13).

Kindergarten

MY WHOLE LIFE I'VE BEEN in training for this. I wonder if any of it is really going to help?

It was the day before the first day of school. I didn't feel nervous at all. I was as prepared as I could be. My lesson plans were done for the week. I had pencils, paper, crayons, and a computer. I had chairs and desks. The only thing that I lacked, besides kids, were textbooks. I didn't have a textbook for each student. I just figured they'd share.

So on the first day of school, in one hundred-degree weather, I stood in front of my door in a light gray suit, waiting for my third grade students to come in. You see, my plan was to greet them as they came in. But no one was coming in. I saw that kids were walking by my classroom, but no one was coming into my classroom! I decided to walk down the hall to see if my colleagues had any students in their classes, and they all did. So, bewildered, I walked back down to my classroom and there was a small group of students congregating next to my door. Finally, a little Hispanic girl emerged from the group and asked, "Are you our teacher?" I replied, "Yes

I am, sweetheart!" And so, she walked in and the group followed. Consequently a number of other students who had been just walking around came in too. That's when he walked in—the son of two of my childhood friends. I recognized him right away because he looked just like his momma and he had his father's name; he was a junior. I noticed it when I received my class list.

As they entered, I told them to find something to do. They just stared. I repeated my instructions. Then some of the boys slowly made their way to the blocks with suspicious looks on their faces. The girls proceeded to the games and the paper. After about five minutes, everyone who had come in was engaged in some type of activity even if it was just talking to each other—all except one. It was the same little girl who had dared to ask who I was. She was just sitting quietly at her desk watching everyone else. I walked up to her and asked her if she wanted to play or draw, and she nodded no!

This same little girl went on to become my best student. She would go on to excel in every academic area, and she was extremely well-behaved. Interestingly enough, at this very moment she was already separating herself from the class, so my first activity was a tremendous success! I had managed to effectively observe the personalities and interests of my students by allowing the students to freely choose an activity, even to the point of identifying my classroom leader!

The rest of the morning went off without a hitch. There were some behavioral problems but nothing major. It was now lunchtime and I was ready to take them to the cafeteria so that the students could wash their hands and eat. What would happen in the next few minutes would make an impression on the rest of my career. As I turned around to lock my classroom door, I heard a collective, "Oooh!" I thought, *Uh oh, what could have possibly happened that fast?* When I asked the children what happened, the students told me that a boy had touched another boy. I'm thinking, "Okay, no big deal!" I asked the students if the boy had hit or kicked and again they said that he had touched the other boy. Finally, someone said that he had touched the boy's private area. This was a serious problem, to say the least. I walked up to the boy, and as I squatted down, I asked him if it was true that he had touched the other boy there. His reply was, yes! When I asked him why, he had no answer.

At this point, I separated the two and attempted to calm the class down, but it didn't work! Now, I considered myself to be a strong disciplinarian, so if I asked the students to do something, then they should do it. They were pushing and laughing. I was so thrown off by the events preceding their misbehavior that I decided to take a drastic step. I announced to the class that they would all be serving detention at lunch, every single one of them! They were very quiet for the rest of the journey to lunch.

The other teachers had no idea about what had taken place, but when they saw my class so well behaved, they commended me on a job well done. Still distraught, I nodded in response to their comments and I followed my class into the cafeteria. I stayed with my class until they went out to play and I placed each one of them on detention, to stand on "the wall."

The wall is an area usually designated near the playground for those students who don't behave. There I was the first day of school, in late August, burning up in my suit, with all of my students lined up against the wall. One teacher asked what I was doing and I told her. I let her know that I needed them to be accountable to each other. Her response was, "You're going to lose your class; you shouldn't have punished them all."

But I didn't budge. My intention wasn't to punish everyone but to send a message. I had made my point because they were visibly upset, and some of them were even crying. So, I said to all of them, "We are a family. Whatever happens to one of us affects us all."

One of them replied, "So if one of us gets in trouble, we're all in trouble?"

"Yep!" I replied.

Another child said, "But what if they just keeps doin' stuff just to get everybody in trouble?"

"Then I will deal with that person individually," I replied with a scowl. "Make sure that you are doing your job. Your job is to learn and if someone is keeping you from doing your job, ask her to stop. If that doesn't work, then let me know and I'll take care of it. Today, no one tried to stand quietly in line. We all decided to just talk and laugh. So from now on, remember that you are responsible for yourself and that everything you do affects somebody else! Okay! Now, all of you may go and play!"

After all of that, the same little girl that spoke to me first, my "leader," came up to me and gave me a hug and thanked me. She followed me around the playground for the remainder of the recess. As she held my hand, she told me about how she had always been in classes with students who didn't behave. She said that she was glad that I was her teacher. She was the only one who talked to me for the rest of the day.

I finished that day outlining the rules and the curriculum. In other words, I told them what I expected from them this year. I also let them know what they could expect from me. When the bell rang, I went immediately to the office to request the files on the two students involved in the lunch line incident and to submit a referral. But when I got to the office and read the files, I found out that they had prior incidents with each other and another young man. When I questioned the assistant principal about why I wasn't given this information, she said that it was confidential and that I was on a need-to-know basis. I couldn't believe it, but I should have known better!

Before becoming a teacher I had worked in the Maricopa County Detention Facility (SEF). There, you weren't given any of the detainees' medical history, including diseases and viruses that they may have been carrying. So, we always played it safe there; we assumed that everyone had been infected. But this wasn't medical, and I wasn't working there anymore. This wasn't jail! As I was walking back to my classroom, I thought, *We don't even have windows in our classrooms. Why should I expect the behavior here to be any different then the behavior at the detention center? In both cases, children are deprived of the sunlight. Would you be happy in a place without windows? If no sunlight can get in, then I will be their light.*

A week or so went by. I had begun to prepare for "Meet the Teacher Night." It was a Wednesday, the day before the event, and I was putting together some information for my parents when a visitor dropped by. It was my old basketball coach and eighth grade language arts teacher. She had now become a district CPT, Collaborative Peer

Teacher, and she was just going around checking things out.

As she glanced through my room giving a nod of approval, she stopped and noticed that something was wrong. She asked, "Why don't all of the desks have the same kinds of books in them?"

I replied, "Because I don't have enough books."

"Did you tell the principal?"

"I told the AP, assistant principal, she's in charge of inventory."

"And what did she say?"

"She said that she didn't have anymore!"

Well, needless to say, I stopped what I was doing and we went to talk to the AP. When she found out that it was indeed true that we were short on books, she left in disgust. I went back to working on the finishing touches: name tags, folders, class rules, bulletin boards, etc. I didn't have time to worry about things that I couldn't control.

The day of the event, before the parents arrived, she returned with some boxes on a cart. She had gone to the district office to get some books from the warehouse. I now had more books, all of the reading, grammar, math, and spelling books. I was still lacking social studies and science books, not to mention workbooks for reading and math. She asked, "What have you been doing all this time?"

I remarked, "Teaching!"

She left with some sense of satisfaction. She said, "I feel better now, don't you?"

I just shrugged my shoulders and kept on working. I'm not sure what she wanted me to do. I didn't have time to worry about materials that I didn't have. Maybe I should have made time.

It's funny because none of that was a big deal to me. Truthfully, I wasn't worried about the resources because I really had no idea of what I was going to do with those books anyway. We have a book for everything! As far as I was concerned, a teacher didn't need all of those books to teach. All they needed was paper and a pencil. And all I needed was a chalkboard.

I know that sounds crazy, but I remember reading an article about Marva Collins. She detailed how she began her first school, in her home. She talked about how at first all she had was a chalkboard, pencil, and paper. My grandmother had talked about similar circumstances that she experienced. She was from Texas, and that's how they did it in one-room schoolhouses, with multiple grades. I had made up my mind in college that I was strive to be resourceful and efficient.

I mentioned in the previous chapter that college doesn't truly prepare you to teach. I think college gives you the opportunity to create a philosophy toward a number of the disciplines within teaching: reading, writing, mathematics, behavioral management, and planning. For me, behavioral management was the most important discipline. When the students are under control, then you can teach them.

I taught math and reading, but I never felt like I was really teaching writing. It was more like I was giving the students opportunities to write and my job was to try to improve their grammar skills, which was very difficult for me. So I taught reading comprehension and math computation, along with some problem solving, with some confidence, and I taught writing from a grammar book with no confidence at all!

I had huge gaps in my understanding of what teaching really was early on. If you think that's bad, you should have seen my lesson plans. My plans weren't bad; I just never followed them. They were very general. They gave reference to the materials and the subject matter but not much else. I also frequently changed the lessons because I was usually dissatisfied with the pace of the curriculum that I was working with. The only thing that saved me was that I took a lot of notes, I observed other teachers during my preps, and I continued to take classes for professional development through Urban Systemic Initiative, USI.

As the first quarter came to a close, I was faced with my greatest challenge, parent-teacher conferences. This was the only thing that has ever made me nervous or uncomfortable about being a teacher. There was so much that had to go into it—their grades, their behavior, my plan for each child, and my ability to communicate all of that.

By communication, I meant speaking Spanish to my Hispanic families who didn't speak English. I had been consistently corresponding with parents through classroom newsletters, informational letters, and informal notes in English and Spanish, but this was different. I was going to have to listen and respond in Spanish on the spot. Even though I was capable, I wasn't that good at it, in my opinion.

My greatest insecurity, however, was inexperience and youth. How was I going to advise mothers and fathers, who were ten to twenty years older than I was, on how to educate their children? Experience, and the wisdom that usually accompanies, was more important to me than anything. My academic expertise was of no comfort to me. American society didn't respect the teaching profession, and I was a first-year teacher. Was I going to get any respect at all?

As the conferences began, I began to see that it was going to be a very positive experience. I found that parents were much more respectful of teachers then I could have imagined. My Spanish-speaking parents were very accommodating in their willingness to assist me with words that I couldn't pronounce or remember. And since I generally had the report cards sitting in front of me, they didn't say much about their grades because the information was there for them in Spanish. But every single parent wanted to know about their child's behavior. Ironically, my parents held behavior and discipline as a high priority, just as I did!

Once I got through the conferences, I felt like a real teacher. The only frustration I had was the fact that less than two-thirds of my parents showed up. But I pressed on. I was feeling better about my membership in the teaching fraternity. I felt like I had taken some positive steps toward being a real teacher with the conferences behind me. But my progress as teacher would be overshadowed by a situation that I thought was trivial. However, it would come to define me far more than anything that I have ever done inside of the classroom, to my peers.

One afternoon, just before one of my basketball practices, the principal called out on the intercom, "Mr. Payton, please come to the office." I froze. My players just looked at me. I didn't move. For a moment, I thought I was a student again. You see, I attended this school as an eighth grader, and if you recall, I've never been a model student. Even then, my principal had this thing about calling me by my last name. So, when he called I had a flashback of being in trouble as a student. I shook it off, and I ran over to the office, leaving my team to stretch and warm-up. (I coached all of the boys' junior high sports.)

When I arrived at the office, I shared my moment with him, and we both laughed. He started off the conversation with a compliment about how well I was doing, and then it came, the "but." He proceeded to explain to me how I had offended many of the ladies on the campus with my demeanor and my antisocial behavior. My response was simple—work and play don't mix. I had already made one mistake. I met one of my students' mom one night for a movie. Nothing ever happened, we didn't even get to really have the date, but my relationship with that parent was never the same. I explained to him that I didn't want to eat in the lounge and didn't want to go to happy hour with them either. He told me that I was making things more difficult for myself than they had to be. I said, "It's bad enough that I'm one of the only blacks here, but the only black male teacher ... in primary ... that's tough enough! Now I have to be a social butterfly too?" He said that I needed to understand that this was "their"profession and that if I was going to make it, that I had to stop alienating the women on my campus.

I finished practice, and then I tidied up my room. On the way home, I thought about what he said, and I realized that I wasn't willing to do what he had asked. Being a good teacher in my classroom was more important to me than being accepted by the female contingency of my staff. Little did I know that this was just the beginning.

As I progressed through the year, I went back and forth on this issue. But before the year was over, I experienced both ends of the extremes. There were times that none of the ladies spoke to me. Other times, I was the talk of the campus, like the time when a teacher I had dated got a little too happy during happy hour and started talking about me. (Your imagination can do the rest!) Let's just say that I learned as much about being a teacher outside of the classroom as I did inside the classroom.

As I fumbled through the nonacademic side of things, I was gaining a great deal of insight to the academic side of the game. I began to get an idea of my scope and sequence—how and when I was going to teach things. The how represented the depth of content that I needed to present. The when is a specific reference to my lesson planning and execution, which was currently very poor, in my opinion.

As I sought answers to these questions, I began to become a student of our school and its functions from the third grade down. With the third grade as my reference point, I began to go into the second grade classrooms, first grade classrooms, fourth grade classrooms, and special education settings. I even sat in on library meetings to get an idea of their inventory and their needs. I went to the bilingual aides' meetings to find out what their challenges were. I sought out the director of our reading enrichment program. I was doing any and every thing I could do to broaden my understanding of what it was going to take to become a good teacher.

As the year began to come to a close, I continued my process of reflection and revision. I was really happy with how I finished the year in terms of my instruction.

My lessons were sharper and more efficient. My students were being challenged, and my classroom was starting to look and sound like true learning was taking place for my students and I.

It was May, and we began to discuss changes for the coming year, classroom assignments, field trips, curriculum changes, and staff changes for our school. I was having mixed emotions about the year coming to an end. Though I was excited about next year, I was saddened by the thought of having to send my students home for the summer. They were my first class, and they were responsible for deepening my love of education and my desire to be a better teacher.

As the last day of school approached, I didn't know what to expect. I didn't know how to pack up my classroom, so my classroom still had most of the bulletin boards and decorations still intact. I didn't really plan my last day very well. I was still trying to fit in a few more lessons. Usually, the last day of school is an abbreviated day, so the kids go home early, but this day was going by way too fast. When the time came, I lined my class up to go home. They said their good-byes with hugs, cards, and pictures. The little girl I mentioned in the beginning hugged me, told me that I was the best teacher that she had ever had, and walked away with her mother. The others piled on to the bus in the scorching Phoenix heat and rode off. I stood there and watched the bus for about half a mile. My principal walked up to me and asked me if I was all right. With tears in my eyes, not crying though, I told him that I was cool, and I ran to the classroom.

I was missing them already. I wondered, had I taught them well enough? Were they ready for fourth grade?

One thing was for sure: this summer I was going to get better! So, I dedicated part of the summer to research and planning. In order to do that, I had to dedicate some time to reflection. I chose a long trip to facilitate my reflection, a Greyhound bus trip to visit my sister in Atlanta, Georgia.

You might be wondering why I chose a Greyhound. Why would I take a long, hot, boring bus ride? I could have flown; after all I had a real job now and real money, not much of it, though. A plane would have been a lot more comfortable. But where's the challenge in that?

So how did it go? It went much like my school year— poorly planned, extremely enlightening, full of surprises from every angle, and very effective!

First Grade

NOW THAT I KNOW WHAT it takes to be a teacher, do I have what it takes to get better?

It was a new year, so I took a new approach. This time I decided to plan my year first. I took all of the info that I had from the first year, along with some of my research, and formulated a scope and sequence over the summer. But that seemed to take a backseat to some of the drama that was building on campus about race and our assistant principal.

My AP was a black woman. She was fluent in Spanish, well versed in curriculum, and a strict disciplinarian. In my opinion, she was well qualified to do her job. I was one of the only people who believed that. Most of the teachers thought that she was condescending, gruff, and unapproachable.

You see, she reminded me of the women in my family, so it never dawned on me that she was doing anything out of the ordinary or wrong. The general sentiment was that she was giving preferential treatment to blacks, thus creating a distaste in the mouths of the Hispanic and white faculty and staff members, which were large in number. With this buzz of unrest about my AP around me, I prepared for my second year of education.

The first day arrived, and this time, dressed in a black suit and a tie, I opened my door and there were students waiting to get in. They were smiling and anxious. These students knew who I was from last year. They had seen me on campus, in their classrooms, and on the playground. This class was very familiar with me. They knew how I did things.

In my tradition of informal assessment, I gave the instructions to the students. They went to the toys and games and books. With no surprise, the boys played and the girls chatted. This time I had two students sit and watch, a boy and a girl. Was it fair to assume that these would be my best students, my classroom leaders? I think you know the answer. This time, I was ready for them!

I called them over to the carpet, and I engaged them in conversation. One was a thin, confidently soft-spoken, Hispanic boy, and the other was a larger, shy Hispanic girl with a bit of a speech impediment, a lisp. As we talked, I found out why they weren't engaged in activity; I hadn't told them to. These students had a very narrow idea about what a good student was should do. However, if given a "direct order," so to say, they would obey it. So I said in a firm but gentle voice, "Please, find something to do." They both migrated to different areas of the room, and sure enough, the boys and girls congregated around them. (Yes, they were my leaders.) I now had some insight as to how to manage this group's behavior—through the nourishment of my leaders.

In my opinion, behavioral management is often downplayed and over-simplified. Often reduced to classroom rules and consequences, I believe that it is so much more. Used appropriately, behavioral management is the mechanism that will allow for creative and unique teaching opportunities such as dyads and small group work, both heterogeneous and homogeneous. These groups will allow the instructor to work one on one with a student or in another small group.

I employed a management strategy that rewarded students who exhibited the attributes of good leaders. The strategy was simple. Students would be rewarded for exhibiting model classroom and playground behavior, homework responsibilities, and attendance. Over time, students would move into levels of privilege based on consistent, consecutive exemplary behavior. The levels were bronze, silver, and gold, in ascending order. Their achievement would be signified by a bulletin board for positive behavior and certificate presentations given at the time of achievement in front of the class. Each semester the students were orally given a list of criteria that would remain posted in the room.

It was a great success. Students were so busy discussing their movement through the levels of privilege that had been established that their negative behavior didn't have a chance to survive. This is not to say that students didn't misbehave. There were still some minor behavioral problems, but the focus was on producing positive behaviors rather than correcting poor behavior.

The first quarter came and went. The second quarter began well, as parent-teacher conferences came nearer. They went well, but I still had some challenges. I had a student who had a history of kicking, hitting, and throwing. He had sustained a few rough days but nothing no major problems during his time in my class. The problem was that my classroom was not my own and all of his time in my classroom was not spent with me alone. I was sharing my classroom with another teacher in a team teaching setting.

Toward the end of last year, we were told that approximately half of our school would be used to populate a new school in the area. They decided to have those new teachers partner with some of us in our classrooms, with their future students. My partner was a petite, soft-spoken, bilingual redhead from the Midwest. We had been getting along great. I taught the subjects in English and she taught them in Spanish; it was a dual-language model. We alternated language and math. She taught social studies, and I taught science. I was learning so much from her. (Thank you! You know who you are!) Unfortunately, my little guy had been giving her quite a bit of trouble.

We had agreed that it would be best that I left the room when she was teaching in order for her to establish herself as a disciplinarian. But it really didn't work. Every time I walked into the classroom, the students would second guess her. For example, if she gave a direction, they would look at me as if to get approval from me. So my little guy would wait for me to leave and then he would "cut up." It wasn't just with her, though!

One day during her time of instruction, the students had gone on to P.E. and I happened to be on my way back so that we could plan and reflect on the day's events. Before I returned to class, I decided to visit P.E. because I hadn't seen them in a while. When I walked out, I saw my little guy sprinting from our P.E. teacher and the

DARE officer. I called out to him, and he jumped into my arms and began weeping on my shoulder. He had been misbehaving, and they were trying to catch him so that they could talk to him. Exhausted and relieved, they allowed me to take him with me.

I wasn't surprised by his behavior during P.E.; I was surprised by his behavior when I got there. Why was he so scared or angry? Why did I make him feel safe enough to cry? He had never cried for any reason, for anyone. From previous home visits with his mother, I knew that this child was impoverished and living in a home where drugs were being abused, so nothing should have surprised me. There's no telling what else was going on in this child's life. He and I talked, and we sent him home. Frustrated and disturbed, I spent the remainder of my planning time wondering what good I had done for this child. I thought, *What was the point of all of this structure and support?* Now I knew that at the end of each day, I had to send him back home, to his horrible situation. My answer came swiftly and abruptly.

It was December, the day before our winter break, and it was time for half of my class, 90 percent of which were black students, and my partner to leave. They were supposed to take a bus to their new classroom, to get familiar with their new surroundings before winter break. As I sat there waiting for the time to come, the students gathered their things in preparation for the move. I was giving the students words of encouragement and direction. I was reminding them to do their homework and to behave. It was tough, but so far they were handling the situation pretty well, but that was about to change.

A couple of minutes passed by when all of a sudden, my little guy walked up to me and said that he didn't want to go. I told him that I understood and that he would be okay. He said that he wouldn't be okay, because no one liked him. I told him that it wasn't true and that I liked him a lot. He said, "But you're the only one who's ever liked me!" and he began to cry. As he began to hug me, I lost control; tears poured down my face and soaked my shirt. As I opened my eyes my entire class, every student, was crying.

I've never had anyone in my life need me the way he needed me. When he needed me the most, I couldn't help him!

It got so bad that I went next door and asked my neighboring teacher to cover for me. With her jaw dropped and eyes wide open, she nodded and I left. I was so embarrassed and hurt. Most importantly, I was stunned by my little guy's words. I had loved him when no one was willing to, and now he was going to lose that and there was nothing that I could do about it.

As I walked back to the class, in a little better shape, it was time to walk them to the bus. Friends walked friends, lumbering together hand in hand. While I walked with two or three students in my arms, he held my hand, voluntarily, for the first time. They all got onto the bus. Still crying, he hugged me one more time and then he stood there, staring. Realizing that he wasn't going to go voluntarily, I walked him onto the bus and said good-bye.

Angry and saddened, I walked with my class in my arms. Like a funeral procession, we wept as we walked into the classroom. The classroom seemed more like a morgue. It was very quiet, and no work was being done; I had no words, no lesson. For about forty-five minutes, we mourned with soft words and long hugs. Finally, it was time to go home. I hugged every boy and girl. I wished them "Happy Holidays" and sent them home for the break. At that point, I'd made up my mind. I was going to be a bigger part of the solution, not the problem. Unorganized and ineffective methods with respect to our students' self-esteem and academic growth would be addressed swiftly and effectively!

During the break, I decided that I was going to bring Christmas to a former student and a current student. They were sisters, and their mother was a childhood friend of mine who had been engulfed in the world of crack. I picked up a jacket for each of them, socks, underwear, and a backpack. I just wanted them to have something to feel good about when they came back to school.

When school resumed, the girls came back with a glow that I had never seen. They were vibrant and talkative, and I was ecstatic. For once, they were showing a high level of self-esteem. About two weeks later, I noticed that the jackets weren't being worn. When I asked what happened to the jackets, the older of the two told me that they had been taken to the cleaners to get washed. When I heard that, I instantly knew the truth and it infuriated me. I knew that she had sold their jackets for a hit.

I signed out of work early that day, rushed over to their house, and began beating on the door. She came to the door and said "Sebby," my childhood nickname, "I know I ain't right!" She knew that I knew what was up. But before I could say anything, the girls came out and my heart just sunk. Both of them were in oversized, dirty white t-shirts with no socks or shoes on, and they were shivering. I looked at them with a sadness that was so deep that all I could do was say that I would see them at school tomorrow and walk away. I told them that I would see them at school the next day.

While I was fighting a war with the streets, my campus was launching a civil war between blacks and Hispanics. The subject was my assistant principal. It seems that despite her efforts to be a kinder, gentler AP, our staff had launched action against her at the district level. Weary from my own battles, I refused to take a side, and for that I was alienated; what's new! Honestly, I couldn't have picked a side. I thought she was a good AP because of her skills, not because she was black.

Despite our loss, my class had rebounded beautifully. They had begun to excel at problem solving, and their comprehension skills had shown a marked improvement. There was a growing problem on a larger scale, though, as I saw it—reading. If you take into consideration the fact that my instructional philosophy is to teach to the top, then it will come as no surprise to you that students who come to me on grade level will excel. The problem is that less than half of my students come to me on grade level.

Specifically, third graders are coming to third grade unable to read. It became evident to me that I didn't know how to teach a child how to read. You might be thinking, *Why is that?* My response is simple: I never had to. By third grade, the list of expectations includes the ability to read. My job wasn't to teach reading; my job was to enhance it.

So I decided to go back into others' classrooms, in different grade levels, to find out where reading was taught.

In a conversation with one of my "matriarchs" on campus, a second grade teacher, she told me to find out who their first grade teacher was and then look at their program. "First grade reading scales are developed, for the most part, in first grade." My question had been answered and a curiosity spawned. First grade would be my next career challenge, but not before I dealt with present challenges in my classroom, this year.

As I stated previously, I was making progress in the classroom. With each success, I grew more confident, more passionate. Outside of the classroom, I became disillusioned by inconsistent practices, insufficient resources, and conflicting interests. As I became aware of these problems, I attempted to address them in my own way. When that didn't work I went to my principal.

We sat down to talk, and I shared my general frustrations with him, and he asked me to be more specific. So I cited our new computers as an example. I wondered why we were getting new computers when we didn't have enough writing paper for our students. His response was simple, "They didn't donate paper!" I'd had it. I couldn't take it anymore, so I went on sharing some of my ideas with him.

As we began to talk, I realized it was his position, the structure, not his personal vision, that I had a problem with. Keep in mind that this man had been my principal as a child, one my first mentors, a pillar in the community. He had given me an opportunity to define myself as a teacher. But as we talked, I think that he knew that it was time for me to move on.

Bewildered, I solicited advice from two other people, both whom had been my teachers and were now my colleagues. They only reinforced my frustrations. They cited tenure as the reason for their loyalty. As I ran out of outlets, I approached a board member. She was a member of my church, so I caught her after morning worship ended. She gave me some financial facts. In other words, she gave me the politically correct response. I didn't need politically correct. I needed action!

So, I took it. In the most difficult decision of my young life, I decided to leave the district, the South Side. Not just the district, my neighborhood, my people—I left it all because I wasn't going to be part of the problem and back then I didn't know how to become the solution or at least part of it.

As the year ended, I knew that I was walking away from my small world of education, in my old neighborhood, at my old school. I was going into the broader world of education. I would now be experiencing the world of racial diversity, middle classes, and better pay, unless I could find a district like my own. I was used to racial strife, poverty, bad conditions, and worse pay. It was a language that I spoke. It was something that I understood.

My AP was replaced and reassigned to a district office assignment, the following year. More computers arrived too! I don't know if they ever got paper. For all of the resources that my school received, they lost two very precious resources, people—one voluntarily and the other involuntarily. I lost something too—my home and my family, the birthplace of my passion, and the shelter of my professional soul.

Invest

Education is the worst-run business in the world.
They ask for more from their teachers,
And they give them less to do it with.
We are bad bankers,
we rarely invest in our own product.
What product?
Our kids!

Part Two:
Reteach

.

No answers, just better questions ...

Second Grade

NOW THAT I HAVE LEFT my family, where do I go from here and how do I start another family?

I've never liked interviewing. Even though I interview well, I've always felt like being qualified had nothing to do with getting hired. For the first time in my life, I was unemployed! I had never left a job without having another job already in place. Who am I kidding? I'd never left a job before.

I wasn't too worried. I had secured some interviews in a district in central Phoenix. So I figured that I would have a job in no time. Six first interviews and three second interviews later, I still didn't have a job. I hadn't even received a phone call.

So I applied to another district in west Phoenix. This part of town had a reputation for gang violence and low-income families. It was near the area that I lived in after I changed schools after my sophomore year. The familiarity that I had with this area was definitely a bonus already. All I wanted to do was to be a teacher. I didn't care how bad the neighborhood was. This district fit all of the criteria that I was looking for.

To make a long story short, I had three interviews. Each principal made me an offer at the end of the interview. Every principal I interviewed with brought something positive to the table. There was one school that stood out.

This school had a reputation for being a good school. It was large, with over one thousand students in grades kindergarten through sixth grade. The also had the most dynamic principal of the three schools, in my opinion. He was a hunter and a fisher, a country boy. He grew up playing sports and he had met me before, and he was a black man.

Apparently, I had trained his daughter at a basketball camp. During this journey through education, I have always worked in the city of Phoenix, parks and recreation department, at many different facilities, in many capacities. At any rate, he remarked at how impressed he was with my knowledge of the game and the way that I managed all of the participants. But most importantly, he was pleased with the impression I had made on his daughter during the camp. I must have been a good one, because he offered me the job before we ever sat down. As nice as that was to hear, I didn't accept it right away.

I had just left home, literally and figuratively. I needed to consider more than just my feelings. I had no intentions of switching schools any time soon. I looked at all of the factors, and this school had everything that I needed. It had a challenging performance-based program for teachers. It was considered to be the highest-achieving school in the district. They were also going to allow me to teach first grade, which was a big deal.

Everyone I interviewed with previously at both districts saw me as a teacher for the intermediate or junior high levels. The reason why I taught third grade at my last school was because my principal said, "They ain't ready for you down there yet!" What he meant was that they, meaning parents and other teachers, might not be comfortable with me in kindergarten or first grade. He made reference to my gender, size, and color, with respect to the community at large. In other words, I was too male, too big, and too dark!

With all of these positive attributes in place, I decided to accept a teaching position in first grade, ESL. I was relieved and excited. I went to the district office to sign my contract. When I looked at how much I was going to make and realized how much better the pay was, it seemed as if I had definitely found the right fit.

There were a few challenges for me. I had never taught this grade level before, so I had to do some research. In addition, I was in the middle of completing a master's degree in counseling; I was close to being done. Last, I needed to take two ESL, English as a second language, classes. Because of a shift in philosophy, the state was moving away from bilingual programs in lieu of ESL program, so I had to complete my provisional certification.

Armed with research and a temporary certificate, I was ready to start my new job. We were asked to attend a school retreat. A retreat—I'd never been to a professional retreat, so this would be interesting. The retreat consisted of an overnight stay, a series of team-building activities, and philosophical lectures that were designed to prepare us for the coming year. I sat back and watched for the most part until our first grade level meeting.

I was amazed at the size of things. Our grade level included eight teachers. At my last school, we had nine teachers combined teaching kindergarten, first grade, and second grade. This school was bigger than I thought. We even had three administrators: a principal, an assistant principal, and a teacher on assignment, TOA. His job was to deal with discipline issues.

As the meeting began, they began to discuss general items. They talked about field trips, book orders, duty schedules, and aides. Aides? We get aides in our classrooms? They shared with me that I would get an aide for half of the day, every day, all year long. I was shocked because I had always been promised an aide, but she always ended up being used somewhere else, for someone else. They assured me that I would get one, but I remained skeptical!

As we began to discuss aides, an issue of language came up. The teachers had a complaint that the aides were speaking in Spanish in the lounge, during their breaks. Someone thought that they shouldn't be allowed to speak Spanish; others agreed. The argument was that if we are trying to teach the students English then the aides should be using English at all times.

Sure, that made sense for the classroom setting, but during their breaks, they should be able to speak however they pleased, so I said something. Not only did I defend their right to speak their language, but I also warned that if someone decided to question how I spent my breaks, generally listening to hip hop or R and B in my classroom, that there would be a problem. And with that I had done it again. I had alienated yet another group of women. This time I had managed to do it before school even started.

After the last presentation, we were asked to reflect. Here's what I wrote:

> The Machine
> "How many engines do we have?"
> There were so many squeaks,
> so many churns.
> Yet,
> it moved.
> As parts of the machine
> begin to move
> others waited for their signals.
> "What is this workable tool?"
> "The last time I checked,
> they called it a school!"
>
> SJP 6/30

(2000 staff retreat)

It was time for school to start, and in my customary tradition, I had on my suit, black I think, no gray! In this case, I was going to have to actually go out and greet my class. So I walked out to where all of the classes were lining up, and there they were, standing in boy and girl lines, with their parents, mostly. So I grabbed the first little boy's hand and the first little girl's hand and we walked to the classroom.

As usual, I instructed the students to find something to do, and as usual, I had a few students sit and do nothing. This time there were about four of them, three girls and one boy. There were a few slight differences, though. These students weren't just sitting; they took out paper and started writing—at least two of them did. The other two just sat. The other difference was that I had a room full of parents lined up along my wall. This was a first grade class, and these parents were still very protective.

Well once I had a good idea of my students' interests, I gave the instructions to clean up, go to their desks, and open their books. I did so in English and in Spanish. As I spoke in Spanish, there was a collective gasp. I spoke again, in Spanish, saying a few funny things, and there was another gasp, a few mumblings, and then some smiles. About forty-five minutes after we had entered the class, some of the parents began to leave. Had I passed? Had I been accepted? Why had they stayed so long? Was it my color? My gender? My height? Or was it just that I was a first grade teacher—their child's first all-day teacher?

By the end of the first day, I had gained the trust and respect of all of my students. I had formally assessed them in reading and math, and I was prepared to plan my year, based on their ability levels. There was, however, one exception. I had one student who seemed to be emotionally disconnected. He was the only student to separate himself from the group every chance he got. He also wouldn't look me in the eye. When he looked at me, he turned his head as if to use his peripheral vision.

So after school was over, I spoke to his mother. I was completely, astonished. Somehow, he was disconnected from her as well. I shared my concerns with her, and I told her that I would be in touch. I let her know that I would begin to start the referral process as soon as I could. Surprisingly, she seemed relieved. I think she was glad to be getting some assistance. I had to admit, he was a handful. The child ended up testing for special needs, but that wasn't the end of it.

For he and all of my other students, my lessons were going well. I was learning how to teach reading from the ground up. I was also establishing relationships with the students and their families. I used my initial assessments to plan when certain skills needed to be taught. Even though it was all new to me, I felt like the students were learning. My understanding of the reading process was growing in leaps and bounds. As the quarter came to a close, I had developed a very good rapport with my students' parents, particularly the mothers. Faithfully, they waited at my door to pick up there children each and every day. Even though my Spanish was a little shaky, I was making attempts to communicate with them orally on a daily basis.

It was now the second quarter, and my frequent attempts at communication had set a foundation for some of the tough issues that I was going to have deal with during conference time. By now, I had built positive relationships with the parents, and so communicating with them about more critical issues would be less difficult. Conferences had now become something that I looked forward to, and they were all different.

During many of my conferences, I was encouraging the children's excellent progress academically and giving them tips on enrichment. One of the things that I stressed was that my students who were doing well be encouraged to read in their native tongue of Spanish. I shared with my parents the importance of their children's retention of their culture through language. Some of my conferences were a little tougher. I had to ask one parent to bring her child to school more often. It seems that the child was so shy that she didn't want to come to school. I warned the parent that she was in violation of the school's policy on unexcused absences. The majority of my conferences were formalities because of how frequently I corresponded with them on their child's progress.

The year went on, and as I approached the winter break, the halfway point in the year, I began to reflect on things to improve on. The area of greatest concern for me was writing. I was still unsatisfied with my instructional skill level. On a different level, I was also trying to figure what type of intervention I could use for my little guy with special needs.

So far, he and I had formed a pretty strong bond, and he had begun to excel artistically and mathematically, in my class. Unfortunately, he had not been as successful with his other instructors. His special needs teacher had been largely unsuccessful with him because of his emotional outbursts and his reclusiveness. The psychologist had been unable to successfully form a positive relationship with him. And our speech pathologist was receiving a very inconsistent effort from him, as well.

She and I had begun to meet weekly. We discussed everything from her frustrations with the schedule to the number of her students. Most importantly, we discussed her frustrations with his inability to perform in her setting and some alternative methods of instruction, including an inclusion format, which we used from time to time. As a matter of fact, the last conversation that I had before I went home for winter break was spent in her office. We spent an hour or so trying to figure out what could possibly work for him. We came up with some great interventions that I still use.

I returned from Christmas break, renewed and determined to reach every child wherever he or she was. Inspired by the conversation on the last day before the break and a few during the break (yes, we work during our breaks!), I was ready, but nothing that I learned in school could have prepared me for my next challenge. It's a good thing that my education hadn't been limited to the classroom.

One of my classroom routines is called "five-minute nap." During this time, I turn of a light or two and I allow the students to calm down on the carpet or in their seats. They may talk quietly, but they mustn't be loud enough for me to hear. Sometimes I use this time to meet with a student for whatever reasons. On this day, I noticed that one of my boys was unusually quiet. From day one this kid always held my hand and talked to me about everything—his toys, his family, anything—so I knew that something was wrong.

I sat down next to him and I asked what was wrong. He told me that his parents had been fighting, so I just let him keep talking. He told me that they were fighting because his father was using drugs. When he said that, I asked him how he knew and he told me that he had seen his dad smoking out of a little glass pipe with white stuff in it. I was alarmed, but I quickly regained my composure and assured him that everything would be okay. He looked at me and said, "I love you, Mr. Payton!" and I told him that I loved him too and that he didn't need to be sad.

I contacted his mother that afternoon and told her that I needed to see her immediately. She told me that she would come by the next day. Needless to say, I kept a sharp eye on the little boy, and I was particularly aware of his father, who routinely dropped the boy off every morning. The boy seemed fine, and he was back to his bubbly self. He was smiling and energetic. As the day came to an end, I was anxious about the meeting with the mother later that afternoon because I didn't know what to expect.

Before he left, the little boy asked me a question. He asked me if I could be his father. Shocked and unprepared, I told him that it wasn't a possibility. "Besides," I told him, "your mom and dad are married, so you already have one." He quickly responded by sharing with me that he didn't like his father because his father hits his mother. He also said that he and his mother liked me better. I rushed him off and took my seat at my desk. As I sat in a daze, I wondered what was going to happen next.

As soon as all of the students left, his mother knocked on the door. I invited her in, and we sat. She asked why I'd requested her attendance. She seemed anxious, because her son had been doing very well academically and hadn't sustained any significant behavioral problems. So I shared that her son had been sad because of their last fight; in an effort to keep his confidentiality about the drugs intact, I shared no more. She burst into tears and began to tell me all about their tumultuous marriage.

As she wailed and sobbed about her situation, I felt like I should have been doing something to comfort her. By now she was standing, but I was a little worried about crossing the professional line. Nervously, I reached out to hold her hand in an attempt to console her. When I did, she sunk into my arms and held on to me as she continued to cry. Noticeably uncomfortable, I slipped out of her arms and allowed her to continue for about half an hour or so. When she ran out of tears and words, I took a deep breath and asked her what she planned to do about it. She said that she couldn't do anything because she was afraid that he would take her other son, their youngest. She also shared that she was afraid that he might harm her as well. I asked her if he had ever threatened her before and she told me that he had. At this point, we had reached a crossroads. She was aware of the problem, but she had no desire to take any action, so there wasn't much left for me to do.

Finally, I assured her that I would do what I could as her child's teacher to make his time at school positive. She thanked me and headed for the door. As she approached the door, I was reminded of her son's comments that day, and I shared them with her. I asked her to explain to him that what he wanted wasn't realistic. With somewhat a smile, she left and I thought to myself, *God help me!*

Despite these issues, this was turning out to be a wonderful year. My instruction had been solid, my discipline strategies had been successful after a couple years of fine-tuning, and I finally felt like I was beginning to achieve a level of expertise in language arts and mathematics. All of this in a classroom with eighteen out of twenty-six students being classified as ESL students, a severely emotionally challenged student (as he would later be classified), a girl too shy to come to school, and a boy who wanted to be my son.

During the year, I was privy to tragedy and triumph; this was one of my triumphant moments. As I said, many of my students spoke little or no English, so oral language was a huge focus for me. I was constantly trying to model proper language with my students. One Friday morning, a payday "casual day," I was dressed in a black Guess denim outfit and some black Lugz boots, which was very uncharacteristic of me, at work. I'm always that "fly" away from work! After I had finished modeling the task at hand and the students were returning to their seats, I noticed one of my boys creeping toward me. He was one of my more stoic little boys. He was hardworking, well groomed, but very inexpressive, largely because of his language challenges. As he finally approached me, he looked me right in the eye and said apprehensively, "Mr. Payton, you pretty!" and quickly returned to his seat. As he walked away, I thanked him and smiled. I was so proud of him for expressing himself to me in English.

Out of all of the gifts, cards, and stuffed animals that I received, for all of the high marks and financial rewards that were bestowed upon me during this year, none was greater than the compliment that I received from that little boy in my class. It wasn't what he said to me. It wasn't even the fact that he said it to me in English. It was the fact that he had the courage to say something from his heart. It was a gift to me that he spoke to me at all.

These moments remind me why I was born to teach. I was born to open up the world to the minds of youth. Every time a mind is opened, my soul is brought closer to God because of the simplicity and appreciation that children bring into our grown-up world, each and every time we interact with them.

Third Grade

NOW THAT I CAN TEACH reading, am I complete? Am I a teacher yet? Am I a good teacher?

With a year under my belt, I felt a little better for this group of first graders. There I was in my charcoal suit, I'm sure this time, heading out early on my way to pick up my class. As I neared my classroom spot, I was stopped by a parent. He was expressing his dislike to me about some of the behaviors that he'd seen during line-up time. I stopped him and directed him to the principal's office. Surprised, he apologized to me. You see, he thought I was the principal!

Once I got the students into my class, I put them through my usual exploratory routine. To my surprise, my boys went right to the games and toys without me telling them to. The others followed. Right then I knew that this class would be special. Even though this class was very independent, I still saw two girls sitting. One was reading; the other was just watching everyone else. When I asked her if she would like to do something, she said, "No, thank you!" By now, I was able to accept her desire to step back because I understood the implications of her behavior. She was probably going to be my top student—the leader.

In my early years of teaching, I was focused on trying to understand what it meant to be a teacher. Now I was focused on becoming a master teacher, an expert in my field. This would be the year that I would fine tune my techniques, individualize my plans to meet the needs of the students, and improve on my ability to relate to my peers; that socializing thing.

With that, I began the year analyzing the students' academic assessments and creating flexible learning groups for math reading and writing. Do you remember when I stated that behavioral management was the most important aspect of teaching? With my management system in place, this cast of characters was poised to give me a run for my money.

Once I began my small group instruction, I noticed that the groups weren't as productive as I had wished for them to be. They were constantly off task, my materials were a mess, and for the first time in my teaching career, the classroom seemed to be very undisciplined. So about a month into the school year, it was time to reevaluate my plan.

> Class
> An opportunity to learn,
> a means of training.
> A soapbox for the needy
> a prison for the gifted.
> Whether it exists
> in darkness or light.
> We never seem to
> make the connection ...

As I began to revisit my ideas, I found a few challenges. First of all, my groups were too large, especially the reading groups. I needed to make the classroom materials less available because they weren't ready for that level of responsibility yet. But most importantly, I had serious personality conflicts.

This class was so much more dynamic than the classes before them. I would eventually label this as my "high school" group, because of the roles that they had been acting out. They were amazing. I had little jocks, class clowns, egg-heads, and then there were those who just went with the flow. I even had some students with special needs in my classroom. That wasn't the problem. The problem was that some of them fit into more than one role. Because of these characteristics, I had to look at my grouping from a perspective that I hadn't considered before. I needed to create heterogeneous groups based on their behavior. Because based on ability, my grouping strategy had been a disaster so far.

So I decided to change my groups. Initially, I tried to separate three particular boys, but then I realized that I could keep two of the boys together. The other one I had to move to another group. My plan was to use the competitive personalities of the two boys as motivating factors because both of them were very bright.

Behavior is everything. Teaching is about modeling behaviors that will equip children with the tools to experience the world to its fullest. As adults, we are trying to model specific types of conduct. Other times, we try to model skills that we hope will become habits. As a teacher, my goal is to model behaviors for the purposes of retention and extension in order to promote academic and personal independence and growth.

One of these boys represented the nightmare that I knew was coming. He was smart, charismatic, funny, athletic, and very stubborn; hardheaded. He was me! He even looked like me, so much so that they began to call him "Little Mr. Payton." In fact, I keep a family picture in my classroom. It's a picture of my family and I, when I was four years old and some people thought that it was a picture of his family.

With the needs of the individuals at the forefront, I made the changes. My groups had begun to flourish, even though discipline continued to be a challenge for this class. With their constant parent conferences and office visits, there was just something about this group. They were fearless! They tested me every hour of every day. But every morning, I woke up excited about facing the challenge of pushing them past their potential.

By the beginning of the second semester, the groups had become very effective. The students were excelling in their comprehension skills. In math, their computational and problem solving abilities seemed to get better every day. Even writing, my Achilles' heel, was going fairly well. I had even added another boy to my class, who was looking to challenge my other three boys for the title of leader.

In reality, they were fighting for second maybe even third place. If you'll recall, there were two girls who chose to sit at their seats on the first day during my exploration activity. Well the girl who chose to do nothing on the first day had distanced herself from everyone in the class in every academic subject, especially writing. The other girl was the closest to her. And even though she was really in a position to challenge her for the top spot academically, the boys were right on her tail. With all of this going on in my classroom, I still kept a pulse on the campus mayhem.

It seems that another black administrator was in danger of losing a job. This time it was my principal. The charge: he was too much of a leader when it came to personnel issues and not enough of a leader when it came to classroom instruction. He was the type of man who could mobilize the neighborhood, including the parents, businessmen, and students. In other words, he was a motivator. However, with socioeconomic changes in the neighborhood and a move toward objective-based incentives based on test scores, his species of administrator was in danger of becoming extinct.

Personally, I didn't see the problem. I thought that we had a great administrative team. Our assistant principal was a more detail-oriented, assessment-driven leader. Between the two of them, I thought that we had a pretty good balance, because too much of either of them would not have been very productive.

Unfortunately for me, the rest of the staff didn't see it that way. And as you read in the second chapter, when the staff speaks, the district listens. Needless to say, he ended up losing his job that year, but before he left I wanted to talk to him candidly about the "other" forces that may have contributed to his demise.

As I sat with him in the principal's office, we discussed his journey and mine. He spoke of his early years as an administrator and a teacher. He spoke about defending his approach toward his position. He also spoke to me about his desire for me to become an administrator. This was nothing new to me. Ever since the day I stepped on a campus, I had been told that I had leadership skills and the expertise to become a good administrator.

Just as he begun to spell out the possibilities and opportunities that the administrative position had to offer, I shared this thought with him: "Every army has soldiers and generals. We are at war with the streets for our children. I'm the highly trained operative that every general needs. I will look the enemies in the eye and defeat them. I don't fear the conflict, and I understand the risks, the casualties that are associated with war. I embrace those risks, and I turn them into opportunities for advancement.

"My superiors are charged with equipping me with the necessary weapons that are needed in this war, but they are removed from eminent danger, the conflict. Your battles are for funding, supplies, requisitions, and personnel. The war that I want to fight is right here ... in the trenches ... on the front line! And I have no desire to leave the front line."

In my experience, my classes have been loaded with as many challenged students as my administration could give me. That's my "calling" to educate those who can't be reached. They're just like me, so I have an insight into them that no one else has. One day I may be "called" to administration. On that day, I will take my place and perform to the best of my ability, but until then I'll teach

Finally, I told him that I that we needed good administrators. But if all of the good teachers become administrators, then what are we leaving in the classroom, on the frontlines? I will find a way to lead. But I will lead as a teacher, in the classroom. Finally, he shared with me the positivity in his situation as we, people of color, have always done, historically. And we wrapped up our conversation.

As I continued to teach the rest of that year, I began to question myself. Though this had been my most challenging class so far, I had enjoyed them more than any other. I felt like I had truly made an impact on these children's lives. They had definitely made an impact on me! However, I did wonder if I was doing enough. I wondered, could I have done more? Was there more to be done?

The answer was yes! With the help of one my students' parents, who happened to be an accountant, I began the process of starting my own nonprofit organization. I wanted to start a mentoring program. By now, I had begun to realize the limitations of the teaching institution. I realized that a teacher can only affect classroom behavior significantly. It would take something more to have a long-lasting impact on a child.

In dealing with my class's behavior, I realized that the change agent had to be the parent. In order for any of the behaviors that I was trying to teach to be reinforced, long term, I needed a commitment from the home. This class was dynamic in their needs that I was forced to get outside of my classroom, physically and mentally. I made more home visits than ever, I had more parent conferences than ever, and for the first time, I had to spend a significant amount of time in the office for discipline. I wrote more referrals during this year than I had written in all of my previous years of teaching combined.

That didn't make them a bad class. As I've said before, I liked this class; they had such strong spirit and who was I to break it? Before it was all over, I'd affectionately given each child a nickname, and they had given me the most challenging experience of my career, and for that I am grateful!

Fourth Grade

AM I FINALLY A PART of the solution? What is the solution? What's the problem?

Throughout my career I have focused on my classroom. I had always taken pride in the fact that what went on in my classroom was protected from outside influences like policies, finances, and administrative changes ... Was I really that naive? *Everything* that happens outside of the classroom affects what goes on inside of the classroom.

This year we started school a lot earlier than we ever had before—the first week in August. It was part of our new school schedule, so our summer was cut short. We would now attend school for nine weeks and then we would have a two-week break. With this new format, we would have three major two-week breaks, fall break in October, winter break in December, and spring break in March.

Initially, I thought that these longer breaks would have a negative effect on my students academically. My theory was that my little first graders would regress with such a long break, as they generally did in the summer. I was really opposed to this "fall break" for two weeks.

It takes about six weeks for first graders to really get it, and I was concerned that they would lose it. As the year went on and the breaks came and went, my theory proved to be wrong. If anything, I think that the breaks helped to rejuvenate my students. I think the breaks provided processing time.

Before the school year started, I took a look at my classroom list and I realized that my class was very young. Many of them were still five years old. If you couple that with the fact that preschool is not mandatory in my state, you would know, as I did, it was going to be a tough start.

As I began my exploration activity, dressed in black this year, I noticed that half of them were still sitting after I gave my directions. As I looked in their eyes, I saw fear and uncertainty. So I took a few by the hand, and I walked them around the class. I wanted them to know that this was their class, and that seemed to help a little. Others continued to sit, so I went over to them and asked them if they wanted me to take them around, and they nodded in agreement. After I finished with the second group, there were three still sitting. Two were reading and one was just sitting.

Unphased by the three, I set out to observe. Just as I was about to sit, my phone rang. It was the attendance clerk. She had called to inform me that I had a student in the office who was afraid to come to my class. Afraid to come to my class; why would someone be afraid? I was just your average six-foot-five-inch, 210-pound black man dressed in a black suit. Most students are intimidated by my appearance. After all, people that look like me either play basketball or are on TV for some reason, good or bad. So, I had come to expect some anxiety, even a little fear from my students.

Fear has been a larger part of my teaching career than I wanted it to be. I knew that my appearance would be an issue for my students; after all, they're young children. Also, many of my students are Hispanic or white; very few of them have been black. Those are the demographics in Phoenix, Arizona. Student apprehension came as no surprise to me. But some of the adult behaviors that I have experienced have been surprising.

I'm reminded of a strange set of encounters with my colleagues. Once, after a meeting that we'd finished, I was walking through a breezeway going toward her. As she came nearer, she instinctively switched her purse to her outside arm. I stopped and asked myself if that had just happened. I shrugged it off and went on my way. That was on a Thursday. The following Saturday, I was at a mall shopping and I saw the same colleague with her daughter. This time, she moved her daughter to the outside and sped by me without acknowledging with any eye contact. I just laughed. Sometimes you have to laugh at some of the worst things. If you don't laugh, you might scream! But that's another book!

As I opened the door, I saw fear. The little girl began to scream at the top of her lungs. She was kicking and swinging, and her tears had soaked her clothing. She was terrified of me. When I asked the mother and the clerk why, they told me it was because I was a man—her first male teacher. I tried to comfort her, but it only made things worse.

By now my whole class was a little nervous. They had stopped playing and started watching. So, I told them to clean up and have a seat. About five minutes later, she had finally stopped crying, but she still was not going to come into my class. As the clerk tried to explain to the little girl how much fun it was going to be in my class, we attempted to move on with the day. Suddenly, out of the corner of my eye, I noticed the clerk was motioning to me to come back to the door and get her. So, I wiped her face, and I spoke a greeting to her in Spanish. I then reached out my hand to her and she took it. Together we walked over to her desk and got her settled in.

As I began to talk, I noticed her looking at the other students. At that moment, I think she realized that if they weren't afraid that maybe she didn't have to be either. We went through the rules and the academic expectations. We completed a couple of activities. By the end of the day, she had become very attached to me. She held my hand wherever we went, completely ignoring our line. When the students asked why she didn't have to get in line, I just gave them a look that said she needed to hold my hand.

We had lunch and headed back to the classroom, with her hand in mine. During our first "five-minute nap," I explained to the students that she needed to be comforted, and they seemed to understand. When the bell rang, her mother arrived to a surprising scene. Her daughter, who had been screaming when she left, was giving me a hug good-bye.

I used the remainder of the week for assessment and training, modeling conduct. After administering and evaluating my assessments, I prepared to create groups. With behavioral factors in mind, I created my guided reading groups, math exploration groups, and some very loose writing teams. Because of the nature of writing, they weren't really teams as much there were some writing leaders. These leaders were used as peer editors for each group.

I had finally found some good writing strategies. More than that, I decided that I should teach writing first thing in the morning. I felt that my students were at their best in the morning, and I wanted to get their maximum effort. I also feel that my worst subject should receive the bulk of my attention. This way, I planned to give writing more time during their best time. Writing was going to be the least of my troubles this year.

As I analyzed the results, I came to some startling conclusions. Based on reading, writing, and math assessments, this class had the weakest academic skills that I had seen up to this point. Add in their age and maturity issues, and we seemed doomed for disaster. But then I thought about my own issues, my life, my journey.

I remembered that I wasn't supposed to make it. I remembered that people thought there was no hope for me. After all, I was hardheaded and undisciplined. I was from a broken home. And according to a statement made by one college professor, I was unfit to be an elementary school teacher, because of my temperament and unprofessionalism. In as much as it had taken for me too doom them, the Lord gave me the wisdom to be inspired by them. But my challenges were just beginning.

About a week before September came, I received a call from the attendance clerk. I thought, *Another new student?* It was another new student, but she was unlike any student I had ever experienced. She hadn't been to preschool or kindergarten, and she spoke no English. We'll call her Izzy. So, I asked the clerk why she picked me, and she said, "Because you're the best teacher for her." Once I thought about it, I had to agree.

A week later she arrived, and she was a handful. She basically came with no skills. So against school policy, I decided that I needed to build a background, some prior knowledge, so I taught her the colors, the alphabet, and her numbers up to twenty in Spanish. I felt like she needed to start learning immediately but that she needed to retain a comfort level because of her lack of classroom experience.

The first nine weeks came and went, and my class was making great strides. They were picking up things at an amazing rate. Their youth had proven to be an asset. Their immaturity had proven to be a positive factor because they were eager to please and very impressionable. My personality was perfectly suited for this situation. I am a strict disciplinarian, but I am silly by nature. I can't help it! So my classes have always enjoyed my sense of humor and imagination.

As we began the next quarter, I was excited about the lessons to be taught and the progress that we were going to make. In my third year of teaching first grade, fifth year of teaching overall, I was very confident about my ability to teach every subject, even writing. I had made great strides in this area. My six-traits scores were higher than they had ever been. This class had been the most impressionable of them all, and as an artist views his clay, I knew that it was only a matter of time before they began to look like a work of art.

During my instruction, I was bouncing and smiling with enthusiasm in my classroom. We addressed phonemic awareness, sight word vocabulary, and writing fluency. We sought out dynamic strategies in problem solving, and we excelled in our computational efficiency. Things were going well. A phone call was going to change all of that.

In one of the other classes, there was a little girl who had been terrorizing one of our newer teachers. The rumor was that she had demanded to be moved to another class. For some reason, my administration was inclined to oblige. So when the phone finally rang, I knew who it was and I knew what it would be about. I was going to receive another new student.

This time, I was in extreme opposition to it. They wanted to move a student with behavioral problems into my classroom. It wasn't that I was opposed to the little girl. I'm a teacher and my job is to teach anyone, anywhere. I was in opposition to the protocol being used. They had labeled this teacher as a poor teacher, more specifically a bad fit for this student.

In my opinion, this child was being rewarded for misbehaving. She didn't want to be in that class. She had stolen. She had been disruptive and very disrespectful. Not to mention, she had been physically abusive to her mother at home. I felt that my school's administration hadn't exhausted all of the possible intervention strategies that were at their disposal. They just wanted to give the teacher a clean slate. They didn't seem to mind disrupting the harmony in my classroom.

So I agreed to the opportunity to teach, despite my opposition to the policy, under one condition. I requested a meeting with her mother. Even though I knew that she wasn't going to be able to help much, I wanted my administration and the mother to know what I was going to do

For the next six weeks, she did everything she could to disrupt and manipulate my students. My class was remarkable in their resilience. They refused to give in to her ways. I spent hours with the family on the phone, in my class, and at their home in search of strategies to make her learning experience positive.

Finally, I realized that the family was incapable or unwilling to consistently support my efforts. At that point, I decided that between God and me, she would be all right. We finished the semester on a strong note, and I went home for break very encouraged!

When we returned from break, the boys and girls came back more than ready to pick up where we left off. It was like they studied during the break. What had really happened, I think, was that everything that we had done had been processed. The rest also rejuvenated them. They were eager and ready to work when they returned.

Outside of the classroom, things were moving in a positive direction. I was gearing up for our second annual Black History Month Celebration. It included a fashion show, history bee, historical recitals, storytelling, and much more. Unfortunately, it would be the last.

This year I decided to involve my class in the formal festivities. So in making a video, I decided that I would allow my students to recite names and recite the works of some famous African Americans. I sent home the necessary paperwork to get permission, and then I filmed the segment. When I came to work the next day, my principal called me into her office. Apparently, one of my parents had called the school and cussed out the whole office and was now looking for me. I made my apologies to everyone involved in the phone call, and I assured them that I would handle it.

As I returned to the classroom, I returned the call. I was confident about my ability to resolve the issue because of the rapport with all of my parents. This particular mother had previously expressed her approval of what I had done for her son, so far. There was a little apprehension, on my part. She was two hundred pounds or more, pierced, and "tatted." Oh, and did I mention that she was a cage fighter?

Needless to say, when I got on the phone, I began by apologizing and then I explained the entire project to her. She made a sigh and then explained her reason for such an explosive response and I understood. The person that her son had been given was Malcolm X. I wasn't even thinking. She and her son were white, and with that information, she had become furious. I completely understood her point of view. I offered to edit his part out, but she refused. She ended by saying that her son loved everything about my class and me. She said that she didn't want to interfere with that! I was relieved to hear it. I had made a huge oversight. Praise the Lord for good people.

With that fire put out, I proceeded with the Black History Month festivities. All of the festivities went well. The video turned out really well. Everything was great, and then I received an e-mail in early March. In the e-mail was requesting a meeting with me about Black History Month.

To make a long story short, he expressed that the administration commended my efforts but that Black History Month had become too big. He said that there were too many things going on. He made reference to the situation with Malcolm X. Finally, he stated that it was taking away from "Presidents' Week." With a look of disgust on my face, I questioned him as to what Presidents' Week was. He made reference to Washington and Lincoln's birthdays being celebrated in February.

I responded to him by stating the fact that we had read a historical minute for Washington. Admittedly, we had neglected Lincoln, but that historical minute was more than we had ever done for any of the Presidents' Days, during my tenure. I stated that these factors were negotiable and correctable issues. Finally, he stated that I would have to narrow it down to one week. I peered into his eyes and said, "It's Black History Month, not black history week!" With that, I went back to my room.

Soured by the conversation, I regrouped and prepared for my conferences. More so than any other parent teacher conference, I was excited. I wanted some feedback from my parents on looping. Looping means that I would move with my entire class to the next grade. I also had to receive written commitments from all parents that were interested, per the administration. Once I received the feedback, then I would be able to share the excitement with my students.

You might be wondering what inspired such a move. Well many things have happened in my career that led to this decision. My experiences, so far, had included student teaching in kindergarten and preschool. I had also spent two years teaching third grade, and I was completing my third year in first grade. My focus is on early childhood, preschool, to third. This was an opportunity to experience second grade. Second grade is where my gap lies presently, so much like I did when I was teaching third grade, I was looking to address my weaknesses within the primary continuum. I wanted to continue to improve, to be challenged, to learn.

Truthfully, though, the reason why I wanted to loop had less to do with factors and more to do with a child. Do you remember Izzy? She was the little girl who couldn't speak English and had never been to school. Well, she did very well. Her language was progressing, she was beginning to read, and she was able to manipulate values in math. Her writing had a long way to go! But I began to think, if had one more year with her, I think she could be up to standard. By the grace of God, the opportunity became available!

Throughout this journey, that started off as a career and became my life's work, I've learned that for all of the politics, social pressures, and financial limitations, teaching was never a job for me. It has been and always will be a lesson in life, love, and sacrifice.

My Reflection

A man is made up of his experiences.
The things that he has done
his present works
and the whole of his future.
As much as this,
he is as good as his company.
My growing up,
included very few men.
I sought them out ...
brothers,
    mentors,
    fathers.
Knowing that brotherhood
(fellowship) breeds strength,
I grew strong from men
past and present.
As I read about them
and watched them,
I am a part of their legacy ...
controversy,
nobility,
ingenuity,
dignity,
ability.
They are a part of me
    and I see them each
time I look in
The mirror.

                    SJP 1/8/02

About the Author

SEBASTIAN PAYTON HAS DEDICATED HIS life mentoring and educating youth people. His 12 year career, in educations, has been spent in 1st , 2nd, and 3rd grade. Sebastian has worked in group homes, juvenille dention, and recreational facilities. His true passion lies in educating and mentoring youth, particularly young men.